How to Dad

HOW TO DAD

John Boswell and Ron Barrett

A JOHN BOSWELL ASSOCIATES BOOK

A DELL TRADE PAPERBACK

A Dell Trade Paperback

Published by
Dell Publishing
a division of
Bantam Doubleday Dell Publishing Group, Inc.
1540 Broadway
New York, NY 10036

ISBN: 0-440-50302-7

Designed by Ron Barrett/Nan Jernigan

Typeset by Sarabande Press

Printed in the United States of America
Published simultaneously in Canada
June 1990

10   9   8   7   6
K.P.P.

QUANTITY SALES

Most Dell books are available at special quantity discounts when purchased in bulk by corporations, organizations, or groups. Special imprints, messages, and excerpts can be produced to meet your needs. For more information, write to: Dell Publishing, 1540 Broadway, New York, NY 10036. Special Markets.

INDIVIDUAL SALES

Are there any Dell books you want but cannot find in your local stores? If so, you can order them directly from us. You can get any Dell book currently in print. For a complete up-to-date listing of our books and information on how to order, write to: Dell Readers Service, Box DR, 1540 Broadway, New York, NY 10036.

TO

Jonathan   Becky

&   &

Gillian   Jessica

ACKNOWLEDGMENTS

This book was a group effort. The authors gratefully acknowledge the following people for their suggestions and support: Marty Asher, Carol Boswell, Patty Brown, Bev Christianson, Lauren Elkies, Nan Jernigan, Ralph Keyes, David Manning, Susan Moldow, Rich Rossiter, and Barbara Schubeck.

We also want to thank Topps Chewing Gum, Inc., makers of Bazooka Joe bubble gum, the Eastman Kodak Co., and the Boy Scouts of America for their unique contributions to this book.

Finally, we owe a special debt of appreciation and gratitude to our editor, Leslie Schnur, who swam upstream to make this book possible and carried us along in her wake.

CONTENTS

Introduction

Having a family is like having a bowling alley in your head. — Martin Mull

For modern dads the birth of our first child is probably as close as most of us will ever come to an out-of-body experience. In that one moment our whole world is flipped upside down, partially by the sheer excitement, partially by the overwhelming responsibility, but largely, perhaps, by the dawning realization that we could actually love someone more than ourselves.

As profound as the feeling of Fatherhood is, it may also be as simple as the three "Dadding Principles" on which this book is based.

The first is the Nostalgia Principle. Teaching our child what we were once taught by our dads brings back a flood of fond memories.

The second is the Peter Pan Principle. You can't help but feel a little bit silly at the age of forty riding a merry-go-round or building a sand castle by yourself. Our kids give us an excuse to be kids again—to reexperience our own childhoods.

The third is the Mister Rogers Principle. Our generation of fathers wants to be more than just authority figures to our kids; we also want to be their friends. Friendship is based on sharing and opportunities, and the sharing of time, experience, and laughter is what this book is all about.

On the following pages you will be reminded of such hallowed How-to-Dad traditions as skipping a rock, baiting a hook, and throwing a ball. You'll also recognize some of the more Modern Dadding skills, such as taking pictures, flipping omelets, and (in the bedroom gymnastics section) flipping your offspring. If you're a little rusty on technique, you'll also be able to brush up on the finer points of handshaking (and high-fiving), bubble blowing, campfire building, card shuffling, and modern shoetying.

Our idea was to try to combine the best of the more traditional role of father-as-teacher with the best of the more contemporary role of Dad-as-coconspirator. The real idea here, though, was to have some fun and to provide some suggestions for enjoying your kids.

Having kids *is* like having a bowling alley in your brain. But experiencing his first bike solo or her first extra-base hit is even better than bowling 300.

—John Boswell and Ron Barrett

How to Skip a Rock

Few things in life are more pleasurable than skipping a perfectly smooth stone across a perfectly still lake ... or more grating than that thunking sound it makes when it heads straight to the bottom. To avoid that sinking feeling ...

THE ROCK

Choose only rocks that are round, smooth, and flat. While you can cheat a little bit on the round and smooth parts, remember: "If your rock is too thick, it'll sink like a brick."

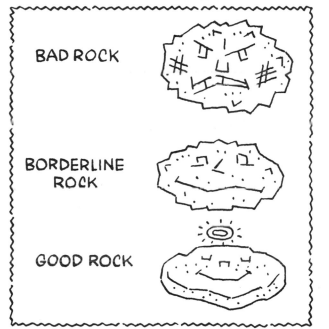

THE SURFACE

Make sure you choose a good skipping surface. A mirror-still lake or pond is best; slow-running streams and calm oceans are passable; rapids and waterfalls are a bad idea. As a general rule, avoid all surfaces with whitecaps.

9

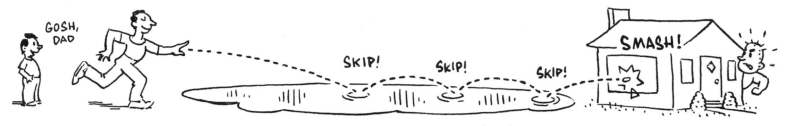

POSITION

Pretend your throwing hand is a little record-player. Curl your bottom three fingers to make the "turntable" and place the "platter" (rock) on the turntable. Steady the stone with your thumb and forefinger, and get ready to make a little rock music.

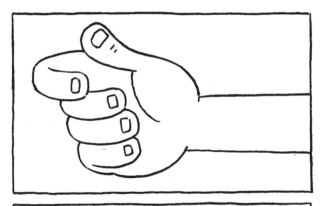

TECHNIQUE

The idea is to make the stone hydroplane its way across the water like a little speedboat. The sidearm throwing motion is best for this purpose, but difficult to master. Instead, bend sideways at the waist and use a three-quarter-armed throwing motion. When you throw your rock, don't think *skipping;* think *skimming.*

10

Note to Dads: Don't show up your kids. Your first two demonstration throws should sink like a rock.

How to Ride a Bike

Sloan Wilson, author of *The Man in the Gray Flannel Suit,* once wrote, "The hardest part of raising children is teaching them to ride bicycles. A parent can run beside the bicycle or stand yelling directions while the child falls. A shaky child on a bicycle for the first time needs both support and freedom, and this is what a child will always need."

Children also need to know they are not going to break into a million pieces. The following patented system is designed to give the child that needed confidence.

CLOTHING

Proper clothing is the most essential part of learning to ride a bike. For the child it should be two of everything (for padding) and especially an old jacket or sweatshirt. For the father, it should be sneakers, a pair of shorts, and a T-shirt. The latter is de rigueur even in the middle of winter, for few activities are more sweat-inducing and anxiety-provoking than teaching kids to ride a bike.

TIMING

Fall and winter are better than spring and summer for learning to ride a bike, simply because children won't complain as much about all the clothing they have to wear and you will stay slightly cooler. The exception, of course, is if there is ice on the roads. Bike skating is even harder to learn than bike riding.

TRAINING WHEELS

Training wheels are probably a good idea at first because they get the child used to subtle maneuvers like peddling, turning, and stopping. However, training wheels can add a false sense of security that may be difficult to overcome later on. A few weeks before removing the wheels altogether you may want to adjust them so that the training wheels are almost one-half inch off the ground when the bike is upright. This will give your child the sensation (however briefly) of what a ride sans training wheels feels like.

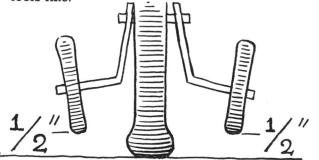

SITE SELECTION

Choose a flat, paved spot of road at least two hundred yards long. It helps if it is not a main thoroughfare and there are no intersections. Freeways and interstate highways are almost never a good idea.

The best site is an underused paved path or roadway set next to a gently sloping grassy knoll. Those are hard to find, but give it a lot of thought and you will probably remember one within a 250-mile radius of your home.

TECHNIQUE

The all-important object of teaching children to ride a bike is to give them a sense of security and a sense of freedom at the same time. This is where the old jacket or sweatshirt comes in. To get started, run along the side of the bike, child up, with one hand at the center of the handlebars and the other grasping the nape of the sweatshirt as though it were the child's "handle." After a few runs like this, graduate to holding only the sweatshirt handle, but make sure the child knows how tight you have it. It is even a good idea to jerk the child off the bike at the first serious wobbling just to show that you aren't going to let him or her crash.

As the child's confidence builds, loosen your grip (but with your hand still in position) until he or she gets the sense of going it alone. When the time is right (you'll sort of feel it), remove your hand while continuing to run alongside the bike.

THE FINAL LESSON

Learning to ride a bike is like jumping up in the air: One moment you're on the ground and the next you are airborne. The problem is that you never know when that micro-moment that separates riding a bike from not riding a bike is going to come.

The key is to stick with it. The first day can be frustrating, the second hopeless. By the third day you may be convinced that your child is destined to walk everywhere.

Then, miraculously, incredibly, for no reason at all, all systems will be go.

How to Bait a Hook

Go back to that idyllic afternoon by the pond: the shadows of fish drifting lazily in the shallows, the hum of dragonflies dipping low over the water, and the horrible, writhing agony of the impaled worm.

Fortunately, worms cannot scream. (Fortunately, for that matter, neither can fish.) So it's easy to pretend that worms have tiny brains that cannot process excruciating pain rather than the more obvious reason, which is their lack of lungs, vocal chords, and mouths.

CHOOSING YOUR WORM

The person behind the counter of the tackle shop will present a bait buffet of things usually found in advertisements for exterminators. Children will prefer a snack. But Dipsy Doodles and potato chips quickly dissolve and float off the hook. Choose instead worms. Not saltwater worms, the creatures that inspired *Dune*.

Not tough, muscular night crawlers.

Choose instead a worm your own size—the garden worm.

BAITING YOUR HOOK

Grasp the worm firmly near its head (the end with the face), and begin to "sew" with the hook until you run out of worm.

FISHING IN POOLS, BATHTUBS AND ACID RAIN LAKES

Only one genus of worm attracts children, the *Plastic worm*. Within that genus the species plastic worm disco is particularly attractive. It appears to be digesting a tablespoon of glitter.

It offers absolutely no resistance to being impaled.

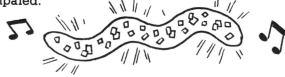

THE ANATOMY OF A WORM

- - - - NERVE

● BRAIN

WE GOT MAGGOTS, SILVERFISH, LICE, NIGHT CRAWLERS, BLOOD WORMS...

CHEESE AND CRACKERS

Snakki-Pak

HOW TO FISH

Once you've baited your hook, you might want to fish.

The method for going after great white varies slightly from that for bream or perch. For the former, see *Jaws*; for the latter, weight the end of the line with a lead sinker just above the leader. Drop in line and reel it out until it touches bottom. Reel it in a few inches to get the hook off the bottom and adjust float to maintain line at that depth.

When you get a "bob," a bite or nibble, *don't pull.* Give the fish a chance to take off with your worm as though he's going somewhere. Now jerk like crazy.

Note to Dads: Contrary to popular belief, both bream and perch (especially white perch) are excellent eating fish. They are, however, difficult to scale and clean, especially when they are less than three inches long.

FILET OF 3" FISH

$\frac{7}{8}$"

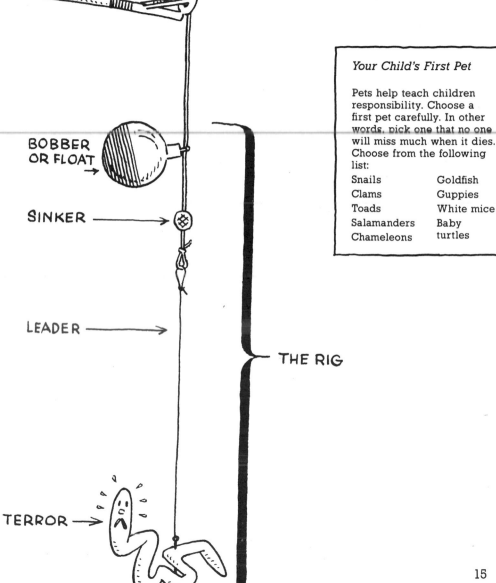

BOBBER OR FLOAT →

SINKER →

LEADER →

THE RIG

TERROR →

Your Child's First Pet

Pets help teach children responsibility. Choose a first pet carefully. In other words, pick one that no one will miss much when it dies. Choose from the following list:

Snails	Goldfish
Clams	Guppies
Toads	White mice
Salamanders	Baby
Chameleons	turtles

How to Play Catch

HEY, PITCH IT IN!
HEY....... HEY...

One of the best things about being a father is that you will have someone you can probably force to play catch with you. Of course, Playing Catch with the Old Man involves far more than merely tossing a ball back and forth. Not only is it a springtime rite, it is a ritual that connects one American generation to the next and should make you feel compelled to build a lighted domed stadium in your backyard.

CHOOSING A GLOVE

Playing catch starts well before you actually trot out on your field. (Some fathers have even been known to sneak a baseball into their newborn's crib.) For most of us, it begins with buying new gloves—one for the little slugger and one to replace the ratty one your mother threw away when you moved out.

The first thing you will notice about buying a glove is that there are now literally hundreds of makes and models to choose from, most with more optional features than a Chevrolet. Therefore, keep it simple: if your child weighs more than you do, buy a catcher's mitt; if he doesn't, stick to models signed by third basemen, shortstops, or outfielders.

PROPERLY BROKEN IN   Mel Catchit   Bobby Blewit   IMPROPERLY BROKEN IN

BREAKING IT IN

You'll be pleased to learn that most gloves are still made from sweet-smelling cowhide sewn together by rawhide that still doesn't stay tied. You'll be positively ecstatic to learn that Neatsfoot oil (sold at most sporting goods stores) is still the lubricant of choice.

To break in your glove rub the entire glove with Neatsfoot oil and add a few extra coats to the pocket. Put the glove on, and with your other hand, throw a baseball into the glove about a million-billion times.

At night, place a baseball in the pocket of the glove and wrap it tightly with a belt or cord. Do this every night for about three years.

PLAYING CATCH

Once you've bought your glove and broken it in, there is very little else involved in playing catch other than throwing a baseball back and forth.

However, save "playing hardball" for the office. It is best to start out with any one of the several soft baseballs that are now on the market, then graduate to the real thing later on.

Even with a soft "baseball" instruct your child *not* to catch "Willie Mays" style (underhand), or to hold his glove in front of his face, as the following illustration demonstrates. If your child never listens to you, see "How to Stop a Bloody Nose." For a little variety, mix in a grounder or a pop fly.

How to Throw a Fastball

MAKE THE LETTER "C"

Teach your child how to throw a fastball and he will think you know everything.

To throw a fastball make a fork out of the middle finger and index finger, and grasp the ball with the fork on top and the thumb at the bottom. For the best grip, hold the baseball either across the seams or with the seams. Across-the-seams is best for small, tender fingers, though Nolan Ryan prefers parallel-to-the-seams and he's done okay.

A fastball can be thrown side-armed, three-quarter-armed, or straight overhand, though the latter is best for control. If throwing straight overhand, remember to keep that elbow up.

Follow-through is the most important part of the fastball. A big follow-through gives the pitch its power and control. As you follow through point your fork at the target. A perfectly thrown fastball will have a slight backspin as it heads to the plate.

HOW TO THROW A CHANGE-UP

It helps to have two pitches, but for kids forget the curve ball, the slider, the knuckler, or other pitches that (really can) damage growing arms. The answer is the change-up and the secret is to make it look just like you are throwing a fastball but—ah-hah!—it doesn't get there as fast.

To throw a change-up hold the ball loosely in the palm of your hand (that way you don't get the same wrist snap as you would with a fastball). Then throw it just as you would a fastball.

HOW TO DEVELOP CONTROL

Good control is far more important than any repertoire of pitches. Remember, it's the child who walks only two out of every three batters who gets to be the pitcher. To develop control select a target about the size of a tiny strike

YAWN!

KRAK!

THE WIND-UP   THE STRETCH   THE PITCH   THE CRINGE

18

zone (the middle of a tire or the bottom of a wastebasket is ideal). Keep your eye on the target and point at the target as you follow through, *but never try to aim the ball.* Now practice throwing at the target about a million times.

HOW TO HIT A BASEBALL

It has been said that hitting a baseball is the most difficult skill in all of sports. But so what? If Don Mattingly could do it, so can your kid.

Remember this four-step mantra and it will make hitting a baseball a tiny bit easier:

1. Choke up on the bat (no matter how big the child or how small the bat)
2. Flex your knees
3. Keep your eye on the ball (*always*)
4. Aim to hit the ball up the middle

HOW TO FIGURE YOUR BATTING AVERAGE: Divide the number of hits by the number of *official* (no walks, no errors) times at bat (example: "Three for four" = 3 ÷ 4 = .750

HOW TO FIGURE EARNED RUN AVERAGE (ERA): Divide the total number of innings pitched by nine. Divide the total number of earned runs allowed (runs not scored as a result of an error or errors that extend the inning) by that number (example: thirty runs allowed in ninety innings, 90 ÷ 9 = 10; 30 ÷ 10 = 3.00 ERA).

PUT ON A GAME FACE

FAKE STUBBLE FOR BOYS

How to Throw a Spiral

It is actually quite easy to throw a perfect football spiral—provided your child is six foot three, 245 pounds, with giant hands and upper body strength.

Fortunately, to compensate for this lack in some of our children, sporting goods companies now make footballs that still have two pointy ends but come in all sizes. Choose a size that a child can "palm" comfortably when grabbing it at its fattest part.

To throw a spiral, the secret is *not* to do anything special to "make" the football spiral, other than grip it properly. To grip the ball, spread apart your fingers and place the last two fingers on the back of the laces. This means your actual grip is about three-quarters of the way back so that only the pointy end of the football is sticking out. (If you grip the ball too far foreward, it won't spiral.)

To throw a pass, bring the ball straight back just past your ear, and follow through as you "step up into the pocket."

HOW TO CATCH A SPIRAL

CAUTION: A perfectly thrown spiraling football can be a dangerous weapon—the pointy end is just the right size for a child's eye socket.

Teach your child from the beginning that you catch a football with your hands—not with your arms, not with your chest, not with your face. Help your child develop "soft hands" by throwing underhand spirals until he or she can catch with confidence. An underhand spiral spirals slightly upward, making it not only easier to catch but also less dangerous.

How to Dive

1. **2.** JUMP!

While there is no foolproof method for teaching children to swim, one way or another most eventually seem to learn. But even when they do, they will not consider themselves "complete swimmers" until they learn the Dive. Fortunately, with one small trick, teaching a child to dive is a relatively simple affair.

For the first dive ever, have the child stand at the edge of the pool, arms extended outward and one hand placed over the other. Now have the child bend over at the waist, head down, until his or her hands are practically touching the water. Now yell, "Dive!"

This is where the little trick comes in. No child will actually "dive." What he or she will do is jump in while bent over at the waist. But what

you say is something like "Great dive!" or "Way to go!"

Now, what you know and what your child *knows* is that he or she really didn't dive, but merely jumped in while bent over.

But now all the pressure is off. With each succeeding dive, the head will come closer to going in first, until *voilà!* just like that, you've got the next Greg Louganis living in your house.

THE ONE-KNEE DIVE

A modern teaching variation is to have the child kneel on one knee.
It is almost impossible not to go in headfirst from this position because it is hard to jump with your knees.

1.  **2.**  **3.**

21

How to Be a World-class Gymnast (Without Leaving Your Bedroom)

There once was a time when you believed the best thing you could ever do in bed was jump on it. Kids have a way of bringing back those moments of unbridled out-of-control innocence. Here are three simple "gymnastic tricks" that let you join in the fun.

EQUIPMENT

The only equipment you need for bedroom gymnastics is a proper bed and mattress. Unfortunately, the better mattresses have become orthopedically, the worse they have become gymnastically. For the tricks described here, however, size is more important than springiness.

The best size, of course, is the king-size bed. From a child's-eye view a king-size bed looks like the floor exercise mat in the Olympics.

If you are a typical married couple with children in the 1990s, most likely you already own a king-size bed, which you purchased about your third year of marriage. If you don't own one, go out and buy one.

Do not buy a platform bed, and at all costs avoid water beds. Not only are water beds a downer gymnastically, they are also passé and tacky.

CAUTION: Before doing any of the following tricks, move furniture away from beds or cover any exposed corners with several layers of pillows.

THE HANDS-BETWEEN-THE-KNEES FLIP

This is one of those tricks you almost certainly did yourself when you were a kid. Teach your own kid to do it as a "bed" trick rather than a "concrete sidewalk" trick.

First, stand on the bed, with the child standing in front of you facing outward. Have the child bend over and place his or her hands between the knees.

Reach between the child's legs and grasp the child's hands firmly, then lift straight up (repeat, *straight up*, not back toward you). Practice until the child lands smoothly on his or her feet and does not complain that you hurt his or her hands.

THE ELEVATOR LIFT

This is the gymnastics version of the growth chart. How long can you continue to elevator lift your own child? And is your child growing all that heavy, or are you growing all that weak?

To assume the elevator position, kneel on the floor (for leverage) with your back against the end of the bed. Now lean back, extend your arms, and place your hands, palms up, on the bed about twelve to eighteen inches apart.

Have the child stand in your hands as though they were stirrups; then, as you extend your arms, attempt to lift your child straight upward. Return slowly to the hands-on-bed position.

With small children, begin by lying flat on your back. Add a "grand finale" by bringing up your feet to support the child, then lowering him or her back to the bed by slowly rising up.

This, the Flying (Your Name Here), is perhaps the most spectacular of all the bedtop tricks.

The starting position is lying on your back, knees up, with the child standing on the bed (facing you) at your (bare) feet. Now raise your feet off the bed and lean forward to take your child's hand.

Gently pull the child toward you until his or her chest is resting comfortably on the soles of your feet. Now lean backward raising the child overhead as you go. Gently straighten your legs (letting go of the hands) until the child is properly balanced overhead. To complete the trick both you and the child, in a mirror image of each other, should spread out your arms in a lay-back (a.k.a. spread-eagle) position.

There are two Grand Finales to the Flying (Your Name Here). One is to continue to raise your legs until your buttocks are off the ground, using your hands to prop up your hips. The other—if you have a Nadia Comaneci in your future—is to lower one leg and balance the child on the one remaining foot.

"Ta-Daa"

It is imperative that all bedtop gymnastics end with "Ta-daa." "Ta-daa" is the exclamation point at the end of the trick that imbues it with significance.

TA-DAA!

CHANGE FALLS OUT OF POCKETS

How to Whistle

BRAP!

"You know you don't have to act with me, Steve. You don't have to say anything, and you don't have to do anything. Not a thing. Oh, maybe just whistle. You know how to whistle, don't you, Steve? You just put your lips together and blow."

—*To Have and Have Not*

If you follow these famous movie directions, the noise that will come out is more likely to resemble a raspberry or a Bronx cheer than a whistle.

To whistle, follow these revised directions. "You know how to whistle, don't you, Steve? Make a tiny hole with your lips, pucker hard, and blow gently through the little hole."

THE FIRST WHISTLE

When teaching a novice to whistle, keep in mind that because of the shape of the lips it is easier to make a whistling sound by sucking in air than by blowing it out. The problem with the sucking-in whistle is that beyond the one-pitch it produces there's not a whole lot else you can do with it. Still, a whistle is a whistle, any way you suck.

HOW TO WHISTLE A LITTLE TUNE

By placing the tip of your tongue on the back of your top front teeth, then whistling *toot,* you can form the basic note you need to whistle a little tune.

Whistle tone and pitch are varied primarily by the dimension of the little hole you blow

through and the size of the pucker. Generally speaking, the bigger the hole and the larger the pucker the lower the note.

Using a modified toot whistle (the first part of the toot but not the last: "*too-too-too*") or your basic note unit, limit your initial little tune repertoire to songs that are in the booklets accompanying a child's xylophone—"Row, Row, Row Your Boat," "Pop Goes the Weasel," "Frère Jacques," and so on.

UnDadlike Behavior

There are certain childhood skills that are best learned from friends:
Flipping baseball cards
Tossing coins against the wall
Thumb wrestling
Choosing up sides
Making spitballs
Blowing the paper off a straw
Making "funny sounds" with your armpit
Noogies

THE BLADE-OF-GRASS WHISTLE

It is essential to learn the blade-of-grass whistle since this is the only beneficial use for crabgrass.

Pick a perfect blade of crabgrass and pinch off the tips so that you are left with three to four inches of the fleshiest part. Point the palm of one hand upward and place the blade of grass flat on the two joints of the thumb. Place the other hand on top (as in prayer) so that the blade of grass is pinned between the two thumbs. Place the upper lip on the upper thumb joints and blow gently on the blade of grass (and through the football-shaped space created by the two thumb joints).

THE BOTTOM-LIP-BETWEEN-THE-TEETH WHISTLE

A shrill, impressive whistle; but like being able to curl your tongue or wiggle your ears, it is a genetic gift that otherwise can't be taught.

THE TWO-FINGER WHISTLE AND THE CUPPED-HAND SEASHELL WHISTLE

These two (also very impressive) extremely difficult graduate-level whistles are mastered by a tiny percent of the population, which happens not to include either author of this book.

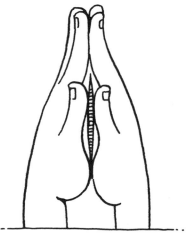

How to Snap Your Fingers (And Other Finger Tips)

Learning to snap your fingers is the first step on the road to becoming the next Tony Bennett or Sammy Davis, Jr. The idea is to create dynamic tension between the thumb and the middle finger. The middle finger is then propelled downward by the release of tension, thus creating the "snap" upon impact with the "resonator," a.k.a. the base of the thumb.

This, of course, will mean absolutely nothing to a child. Try this:

1. Make a fist. Now raise the middle finger (the forefinger will raise also) and place it on top of your thumb.
2. Use the top joint of your middle finger to mash down your thumb. (From the side it should look like a little dragon resting its chin on your thumb.)

3. While continuing to mash, let the middle finger slip down the little slide part of your thumb until it slips off and comes crashing down on the fingers below.

FINGER-POPPIN' TIME

Learning to snap your fingers begs the question "Now what?" Here's the short list:

1. Keeping time to the music.
2. Indicating ease ("It's a snap"), or speed ("in a snap").
3. Choreographing dance routines—e.g., the Temptations' first movement to "My Girl."
4. Telling a joke: Move your arm in a big circle, snapping your fingers as you go and ask, "What's this?" Answer: "A butterfly with hiccups."
5. Making a horse clipclop sound (snap—snap—slap).

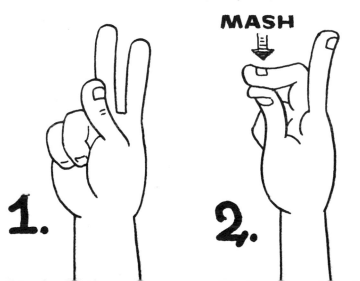

MASH

1.   **2.**

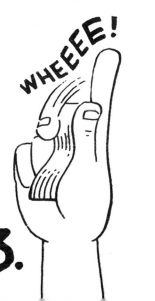

WHEEEE!

3.

SNAP!

4.

FINGER TRICKS

HERE'S THE CHURCH

(It's amazing how long it takes little kids to figure this one out.)

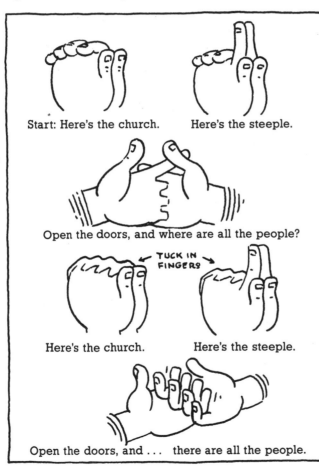

Start: Here's the church.　　Here's the steeple.

Open the doors, and where are all the people?

TUCK IN FINGERS

Here's the church.　　Here's the steeple.

Open the doors, and ... there are all the people.

THE POPPING CORK

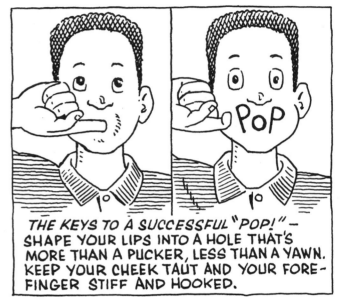

POP

THE KEYS TO A SUCCESSFUL "POP!" — SHAPE YOUR LIPS INTO A HOLE THAT'S MORE THAN A PUCKER, LESS THAN A YAWN. KEEP YOUR CHEEK TAUT AND YOUR FORE-FINGER STIFF AND HOOKED.

THE MOVABLE THUMB

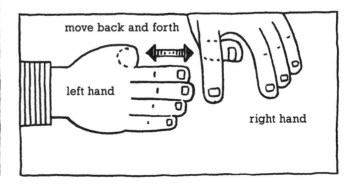

move back and forth

left hand

right hand

THE FINGER WIGGLE

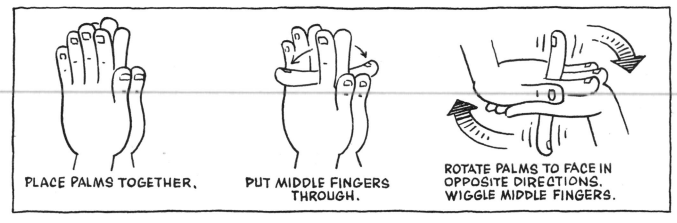

PLACE PALMS TOGETHER.

PUT MIDDLE FINGERS THROUGH.

ROTATE PALMS TO FACE IN OPPOSITE DIRECTIONS. WIGGLE MIDDLE FINGERS.

FLY AWAY HOME

Two little blackbirds
Sitting on a hill
DRAW FACES ON POINTER FINGERS

One named Jack
And one named Jill
SHOW MIDDLE FINGERS

Fly away, Jack
Fly away, Jill

Come back, Jack
Come back, Jill
SHOW POINTER FINGERS

How to Shake Hands

No child—male or female—should be allowed to enter adulthood with a wimpy handshake. A wimpy handshake has been known to lose jobs and destroy careers. A firm, steady handshake is what you use to greet big shots and close Big Deals.

THE GRIP

The grip, of course, is the most important part of the handshake. It should be firm but not viselike, though almost any degree of firmness is better than one of those wet-noodle efforts.

Be aware that children of the male persuasion will often use firmness as an excuse to wrestle the shakee to the ground. To avoid extremes use the same maxim that applies to holding a golf club or a tennis racquet: Grip it as though you were holding a bird—firm enough to keep it from flying away but not so tight as to crush it.

Shake hands firmly and steadily but only for two or three pumps (four pumps at the most, but only if you are extraordinarily happy to meet someone). Avoid exaggerated water-pump motion.

EYE CONTACT

When shaking hands it is often good form to smile, to say something pleasant like "Nice to meet you," and to look the other person in the eye.

When teaching children to shake hands do not insist on the eye contact part. It is easier to get a child to eat oat bran than to look another person (especially a stranger) straight in the eye. Just let them know that this is part of the ritual and one day they might want to incorporate eye contact into their repertoire.

FIVES, HIGH AND LOW: A SAMPLER

These days, possessing a traditional firm handshake may not be enough. While the media has yet to report that Donald Trump closed a big deal by jumping in the air and slapping a high five on his partner, it helps to have at least a passing knowledge of recent high-fiving trends.

REGULAR FIVE: REGULAR TEN

GIMME FIVE AND SHOW YOU'RE ALIVE!

Note: Regular fives and tens usually come in pairs, one up and one down.

WRONG

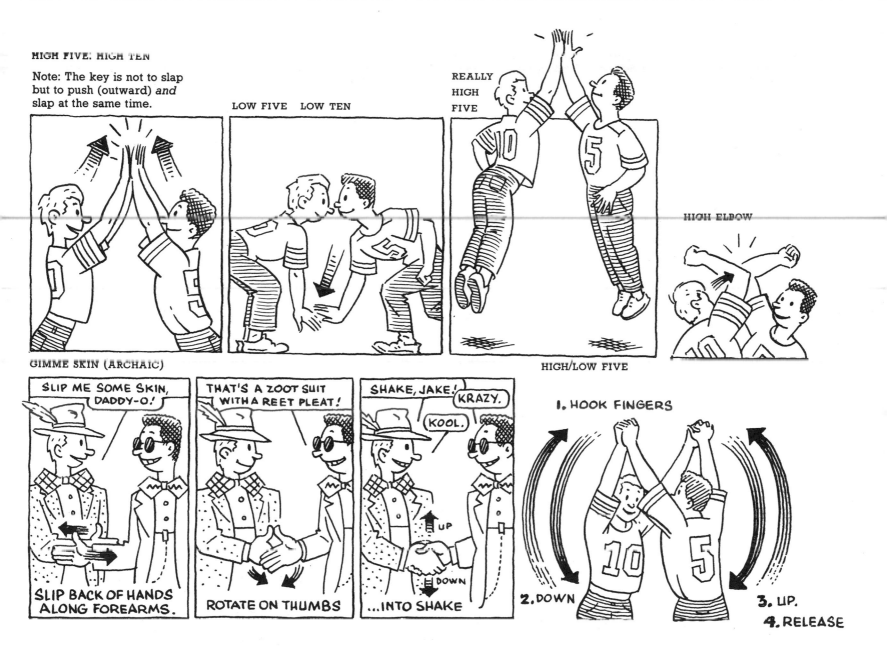

How to Tie a Tie

For any boy a necktie provides an important function: It keeps a strip of shirt entirely free from stains. It is also decorative and emblematic. It is the banner that flies from the pole of the lad.

It should, therefore, be chosen carefully. Ties for boys should not have pictures of female nudes, cocktail glasses, or advertising slogans on them. Club patterns or rep stripes are boring but best.

Begin with the fat end of your tie on the left, and the skinny end on the right. The fat end should be twice as long as the skinny one. Now wrap the fat end over the skinny end. Bring it behind the skinny end and wrap it over itself. Then bring it across the embryonic knot, behind and up through the "V" formed by both ends.

Bring the fat end down through the tunnel created over the skinny end. Tighten by holding the embryonic knot in one hand while pulling down on the skinny end with the other hand. Fiddle with it till it looks right.

TROUBLESHOOTING

Our society is founded on the premise that the fat end of a necktie shall be slightly longer than the skinny one. If it doesn't come out that way, either start over or stick the skinny end in your pants. Unless, of course, you happen to be wearing shorts.

How to Tie Shoes

Look at that kid with his fishing pole (see "How to Bait a Hook," page 14). He sure is cute: tousled hair, freckled cheeks, shoelace untied.

Now look—he's tripped over that shoelace (see "How to Stop a Bloody Nose," page 59). Sure, Velcro could've saved him, if he *had* Velcro. What he needed, of course, was some solid shoe-tying know-how.

THE BUNNY EARS METHOD

The easiest way to tie a shoe is to use the Bunny Ears Method. It's best practiced with the shoe off the foot or on a shoe simulator, which you can make from the box your child's shoes came in.

SHOE SIMULATOR

Begin by making an overhand knot.
Then make the two ears.
Cross them to make Bunny Ear Tunnel.
Bring the topmost ear around the back of the tunnel and through. It's a second overhand knot.
Ignore animal-rights groups and tighten the knot by pulling on the bunny's ears.

The Double Knot

You can turn it into a double knot by bringing the ear around and through the tunnel for a second time.

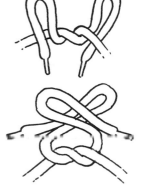

HOW TO GIVE A SPIT SHINE

It may have been Buster Brown who said: "The shoes are the mirrors of the soul." It was certainly our National Armed Forces that made the "spit shine" a habitual ritual. To give your shoes a good spit shine:

1. Remove lid from a can of wax polish that is approximately the color of your shoes.
2. Wipe soft cloth folded to several thicknesses across surface of wax.
3. Allow to dry while working up a mouthful of saliva.
4. Buff shoes with a soft cloth. (Use the same cloth over and over again until it becomes your special ultra-soft cloth.)
5. Expectorate onto shoe tips and continue to buff.
6. Admire high gloss.

The inquiring mind may ask, "Why spit? Isn't it very rude to shine shoes in this manner?"

The answer is it may be. But saliva contains a silicone-like substance that scientists simply have not been able to duplicate artificially.

How to Tell a Joke

As writer, lyricist, and four-time father Sean Kelly once noted, dads love to bore their kids with jokes and kids love to torment their dads with riddles.

Telling a joke is a child's introduction to "structured" humor as practiced by Henny and Rodney; it introduces the child to such sophisticated concepts as the Setup, the Punch Line, Not Giggling, and Laughing in the Right Places.

Generally a child's early attempt at telling a joke goes like this: "Dad, you gotta hear this riddle. This is *so* funny. Okay? Okay? Okay. 'Why . . .' Okay, wait. Let me start over. Okay. 'Why did the chicken . . .' (giggle) Okay, wait. This is just *so* funny . . . Have you heard this before?"

TRAINING JOKES

You have to learn to walk before you can run, and just as in learning to ride a bike "training jokes" can sometimes help.

We have chosen for this purpose three cemetery jokes because every time you travel in a car you tend to pass thousands of cemeteries, thus giving your child *ample* opportunity to try out his or her material.

The first joke is a one-liner, not even requiring a setup. As the car passes a cemetery the child looks out the window and exclaims, "Look at all the dead people!"

Everyone in the car will turn their heads, see the cemetery, and die laughing as your child basks in the glow of his or her own macabre cleverness.

The next two jokes help teach two fundamental tenets of joke telling: (1) *timing:* between the time you ask the question and the time you give the answer, *wait for the person to say, "I don't know";* and (2) *not telegraphing:* telling someone how funny a joke is going to be makes it *less funny rather than more funny.* (There are some grown-ups you might want to remind of this as well.)

35

Joke 2: Why are there fences around cemeteries?
Because people are dying to get in.

Joke 3: Why did the little (boy/girl) refuse to enter the cemetery?
Because (he/she) wouldn't be caught dead there.

STAND-UP COMEDY

Once your child has mastered a few fundamental jokes, he or she will rapidly want to advance to the lounge-lizard phase of his or her comedy career. The following routine is stand-up comedy's version of Chopsticks. It is used to hone such stand-up comedy skills as the Pregnant Pause, the Look, and Eye Contact with the Audience. As a study aid the Pauses and Half Pauses have been added:

"Hello, ladies and germs. (Pause) I just flew in from the Coast. (Half Pause) Boy, are my arms tired. (Pause) Lemme tell ya, it was raining cats and dogs out there. (Half Pause) I kept stepping in poodles. (Pause) No, but seriously folks. (Half Pause) Do you want to hear a dirty joke? (Half Pause) A white horse fell in a mud puddle. (Pause) Speaking of puddles, I saw a magic trick today. (Half Pause) A man walking down the street turned into a coffee shop. (Pause) I'm tellin' ya, it's a crazy world out there. (Half Pause) Take my dad. (Half Pause) Please. (Pause) Thank you. You've been a wonderful audience. (Wave) Just great. (Wave) Just great. (Wave)."

How to Dance

Your kids do not wish to learn any of your old-fogey dances like the Twist or the Jerk, at least not from you. In fact, in the paradoxical world of generational gap-bridging the only really cool parental dances are those so monumentally uncool, they go full circle and become cool again.

From the land of a thousand dances, here are four:

1. Stare straight ahead with a big stupid grin on your face.
2. Bounce up and down slightly but continuously and rapidly (about four times a second).
3. Now, in time to the music, place the fingers of one hand on your stomach while sticking out (palm) of your other hand.
4. Rapidly move alternate hands back and forth, all the while bouncing up and down with that stupid grin on your face.

1. Stare straight ahead with a big *vacant* (Steve Martinish) grin on your face.
2. Lean back slightly, point your two index fingers upward, and twist to the music.

THE WANDERING KNEECAP

1. **2.**

3. **4.**

(works best with two-year-olds or younger)

1. Place left hand on left knee, right hand on right knee.
2. As you bring knees together, cross hands and leave them in this position as you move your knees apart.
3. Cross back when the knees come together again.
4. Smooth out the act so that it actually looks like it is your knees that are switching places and not your hands.

THE DAD TWO-STEP

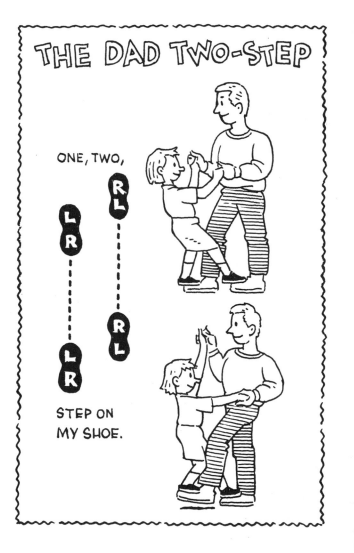

ONE, TWO,

STEP ON MY SHOE.

How to Shuffle Cards

Shuffling cards is no big deal except when all your friends can do it and you can't. Avoid the heartbreak of peer pressure by turning your child into a card sharklet now.

THE STACKING-THE-DECK SHUFFLE. Cut the deck five or six times. Restack the cards, placing the bottom pile on the next-to-bottom pile, and so on, until the entire deck has been restacked. Repeat two or three times.

THE KINDA-MUSH-'EM-TOGETHER SHUFFLE. Cut the deck and hold each half loosely in each hand. Now kinda mush 'em together. Do this several times.

THE SHUFFLE SHUFFLE. The real shuffle is a bit difficult for small hands. Start with the smaller than usual cards that often come with kids' games. Practice with two (gummed-edged) notepads until the sharklet gets the "feel" of the shuffle.

With actual cards, cut the deck in the middle and grasp the two stacks lengthwise (widthwise if your child's fingers don't fit) with your two hands. Reverse one of the stacks so that both stacks are facing inward.

Tamp the cards on the playing surface to stack them evenly. Now use your thumb and forefinger to bow the backs of each stack (see illustration).

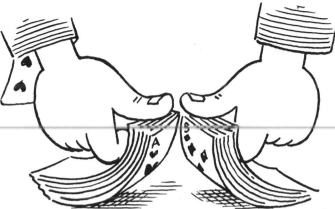

Hold the stacks on a diagonal so that the corners are almost touching. Now, using a thumb and forefinger action, fan the cards downward so that the falling cards from the two stacks overlap with one another. Stack and start again.

FLIPPITY FLIPPITY FLIP

THREE CARD GAMES

WAR (OR BATTLE). War is a game for two people. people. Deal half a deck (twenty-six cards) to each player. Begin by having each player simultaneously turn over the top card in his pile. The higher cards "wins" both cards, and the winner then places the two cards at the bottom of his pile. Play continues in this manner until the turned cards are a pair. Now we have a "war." The pair remains in the center and each

player then turns an additional card, with the higher card winning all four cards. (If the second set of turned cards is also a pair, a third set of cards is turned. The higher card wins all six cards.) When you stop play, the player with the most cards wins.

CONCENTRATION. On a large table lay out an entire deck of cards facedown. The first player then flips over any two cards, one at a time. If they are a pair, the player takes them and continues his turn by flipping over two more cards. If the cards turned over are not a pair, they must be turned back facedown. It is now the next player's turn.

The idea is to remember what cards have been turned up previously and to match them when it is your turn. The player to match the most cards and collect the most pairs wins.

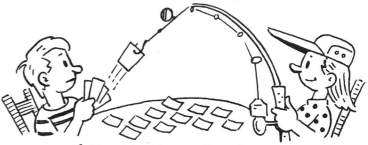

GO FISH! The object is to collect the most sets of four cards of the same rank or number. Deal seven cards to each player (five cards if more than two are playing) and place the rest of the pack facedown in the middle of the table. (This is the "stock pond.")

Each player in turn asks one of the other players to match a numbered card he is already holding—for example, "Do you have any fives?" The player who is asked must relinquish all cards he is holding of that number. If he has none, the player whose turn it is, is then told to "go fish" from the stock pond. A player's turn continues as long as he is successful in obtaining his asked-for cards, either from another player or from the stock pond.

Whenever a player collects four cards of the same rank, he places them faceup in front of his hand. The player with the most sets wins.

How to Flip a Coin, Find It in Your Ear, or Catch It off Your Elbow

Flipping a coin would seem to be one of those things you were born knowing how to do. While it's hardly brain surgery (or even skipping a rock), there still are a few things you'll need to know.

For the simplest flipping method, refer to the "How to Skip a Rock" illustration, which, for your ease and comfort, has been painstakingly redrawn here. Now simply place the thumb *under* the coin (and snugly against the coiled forefinger) rather than next to it, as with the rock.

The coin itself should be of a large enough denomination (a quarter or more), and it should be placed so that the center of the coin rests on the forefinger and not over the thumb. (It is this "off-centeredness" that imparts the spin.)

Use the pressure of the thumb against the curved forefinger to create an upward spring action with the thumb. Now *flip*!

UNSKILLED COIN TRICKS

Kids, for the most part, don't like coin tricks. If it's too complicated, they lose interest; if it's easy, they want to know how to do it, discover there is skill and practice involved ... and lose interest.

The only acceptable coin tricks are unskilled coin tricks. The world's easiest and stupidest unskilled coin trick, of course, is the old coin-in-the-ear bit. Conceal a coin in your hand and say, "Oh, look what I found in your ear!" (or, "What's in your ear?"). Place your hand—*the one with the coin in it*—next to the child's ear, pull it away, and show the child the coin.

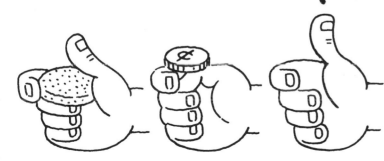

41

HOW TO SPIN A QUARTER (RIGHT HANDED) — HOLD THE COIN ON ITS EDGE WITH YOUR LEFT FOREFINGER. GIVE GEORGE A HARD FLICK BEHIND THE HEAD WITH YOUR RIGHT FOREFINGER.

FLICK HERE

BUT I GET DIZZY

MARTHA, HELP!

Mind-boggling as it might seem, that is the entire trick.

On a slightly higher cerebral plane you might want to try the catch-the-coin-off-your-elbow routine. First raise your elbow so that your forearm is parallel to the floor. Now place a quarter—or even a stack of quarters—on your elbow. The idea is to try to catch the quarter(s) in your hand as you bring your elbow down.

This is actually a very good trick because it involves a BIG SECRET, without knowledge of which the coins will invariably go crashing to the floor and bounce all over the place.

The BIG SECRET is this: Do not try to catch the coins. As you bring your arm down, *try to catch your "elbow"* (or the spot where your elbow was) *by flexing your knees.*

A few practice tries applying the BIG SECRET and it will be hard to imagine that there was ever a time when you could not catch a coin off your elbow.

THE BIG SECRET

42

How to Make Hand Shadows

Before there was TV there was the...

DOG: I'M HUNGRY, LET'S GET A TURKEY SANDWICH.
RABBIT: OKAY.

RABBIT: THERE'S ONE NOW! IN THE GRASS!

DOG: PUT THE BREAD ON HIM, QUICK!

BOTH: OH PHOOEY! HE FLEW AWAY!
THE END.

Of all the great things to do in the dark, hand shadows are right up there with sleeping. What a source of wonderment it is to see how out of a tangled and knotted mass of fingers can come something beautiful, like the profile of a turkey.

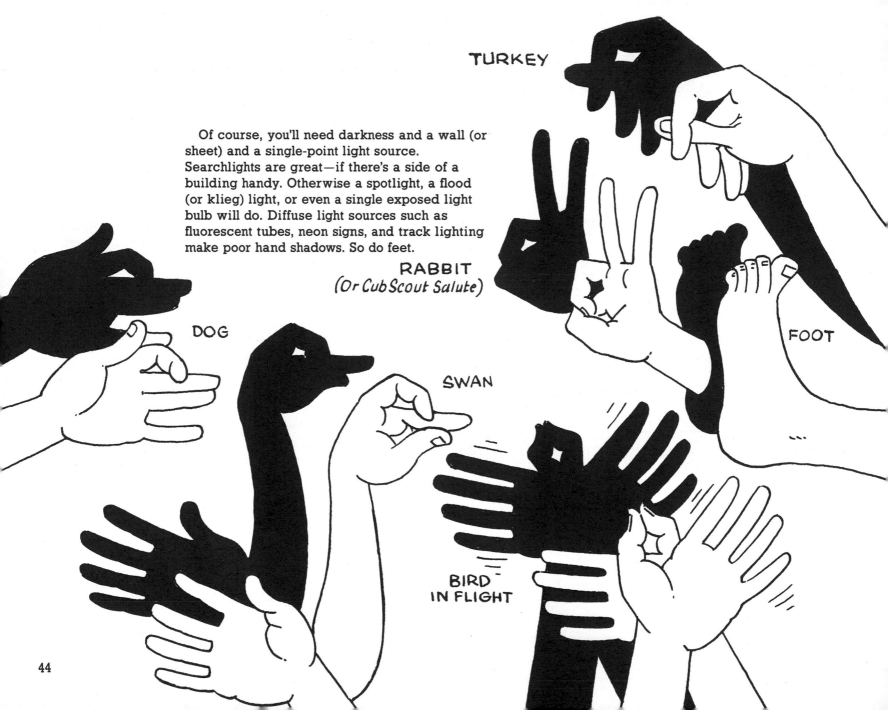

TURKEY

Of course, you'll need darkness and a wall (or sheet) and a single-point light source. Searchlights are great—if there's a side of a building handy. Otherwise a spotlight, a flood (or klieg) light, or even a single exposed light bulb will do. Diffuse light sources such as fluorescent tubes, neon signs, and track lighting make poor hand shadows. So do feet.

RABBIT
(Or Cub Scout Salute)

FOOT

DOG

SWAN

BIRD
IN FLIGHT

How to Lose at Tic Tac Toe (and Play Monopoly in Less Than Five Hours)

It is quite extraordinary that tic-tac-toe has survived, indeed thrived, through the ages, when you consider that technically, every game ever played should have ended in a tie (a.k.a. "Cat").

It has endured almost in spite of itself because it is simple to play, can be played almost anywhere, and can be easily lost to a child.

The easiest way to lose at tic-tac-toe is simply not to pay attention. Your child may soon tire of this tactic (which may be the point), in which case you might want to teach him The Trap. To employ The Trap the child must go first and place his or her x or o in one of the corner boxes. You in turn must *not* place your first x or o in the center. The damned-if-you-do-damned-if-you-don't trap has now been set. Two correct child-moves later, and you're a dead duck.

CHILD'S MOVE   YOUR MOVE   THE TRAP

HOW TO PLAY MONOPOLY IN LESS THAN FIVE HOURS

On a related subject, when you rediscover Monopoly through your kids, you will be surprised to learn that the game has no real ending, considering how long you have to play before a clear winner can be declared.

The game is interminable. For some reason this never seemed to bother us when we were kids, but it can be terribly disconcerting now, particularly if you have something else you need to do during this particular lifetime. (Notice that your parents never played Monopoly with *you*.)

It must have bothered someone else as well because now a "quicker" version of Monopoly has been incorporated into the official rules.

Begin by shuffling the property cards and dealing them to the players. Now trade your Park Place for one Utility and Ventnor Avenue and so on. Right there you've cut the first ninety minutes off the game. You want to bring the game down to under three hours? Set a time limit.

Note to Dads: You wonder if your child's inability to lose gracefully is typical behavior or unique to your kid. Relax. Almost no kids know how to lose; even a lot of forty-year-old kids.

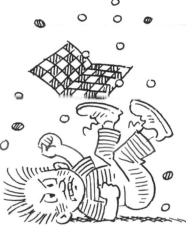

How to Blow a Bubble

"Le plus bubble gum change, le plus bubble gum c'est la même chose." It still comes in distinctive colors, usually hot pink or passionate purple and classic shapes: gumball round, trading card slab, and traditional quasi-cubic. There is the occasional new gimmick shape (shredded in a pouch or rolled flat like tape) but once between the teeth all bubble gum looks pretty much the same.

"Bubble" gum, as opposed to "chewing" gum, exists primarily for the purpose of blowing bubbles. Don't waste your time trying to blow a bubble with chewing gum. It can be done but only after it has been allowed to set on the bedpost overnight. By contrast, bubble gum, at the usual rate of one mastication per second, will achieve sufficient elasticity in two or three minutes.

THE ELEMENTARY METHOD

The easiest method for blowing a bubble is actually not the correct method. But for novices, the sensation of blowing a bubble is often more important than proper technique.

1. Place the chewed wad between your palms and press the gum flat. Forgetting to wash your hands before this step will dramatically demonstrate bubble gum's unique deep-pore cleansing qualities, with the result being very pink palms and a very gray gum.
2. Place the flattened wad under your lips but *over* your teeth (as opposed to the more conventional behind-the-teeth position.) Use your hands to hold the gum in place.
3. Form a pocket in the middle of the gum with your tongue and then blow into this pocket. Be careful to leave a small hole between your lips. Otherwise, the gum may implode and leave deposits on the medulla, the retinal nerve and the bones of the inner ear.

X-RAY SHOWING BACK-BLASTED BUBBLE HANGING FROM BASE OF BRAIN. *NOTE SCATTERING OF TEETH.*

THE ADVANCED METHOD

At this point, we take great pleasure in introducing the world's greatest authority on bubble blowing, a great talent, a wonderful guy and a very dear friend—Mister Bazooka Joe himself.

46

How to Make French Toast

The best part of making French toast is the chance to stick your fingers into a pile of egg-bloated bread. Care must be taken to select a loaf with the proper absorbency factor. Avoid twenty-five-grain sprouted oat bran European health loaves. They are slow on the egg uptake. Choose instead a bread with the heft and feel of a bag of cotton balls.

Scramble eggs in a flat-bottomed bowl, about one egg for two slices of bread. Your child will note with revulsion the long, slimy, clear things in the eggs. These are chalazae, which the dictionary defines as long, slimy, revolting clear things. Add a few splashes of milk (one tablespoon per egg) and some cinnamon or vanilla for flair.

SELECTING THE PROPER LOAF

basement. Place the "building" into the egg mixture. When the basement gets flooded with egg, place it on the roof. Continue this process until the whole house is flooded. Turn the whole mess upside down and do it again.

Separate the floors and place them in a well-oiled, well-heated pan. This part is pretty dull. It's where the bread gets brown and cooked, or black and burned, depending upon your attention span.

Flipping provides some relief from the boredom. It may be compared to turning a doorknob, as the rotation is from the wrist. A full-arm rotation will cause the toast to leave the immediate vicinity of the pan.

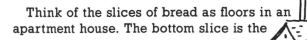

Think of the slices of bread as floors in an apartment house. The bottom slice is the

Serve with butter and lots of syrup.

CAUTION: Do not attempt to make a side dish like bacon or cantaloupe (especially bacon and eggs). It is not possible to make French toast and do anything else simultaneously.

How to Make an Omelet

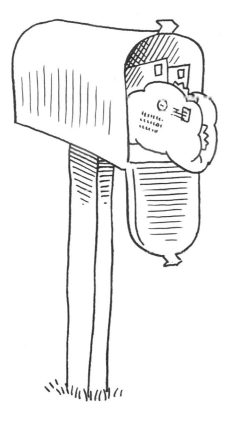

AN OMELET IS AN EGG ENVELOPE.

An omelet is simply French toast without the bread, the vanilla, and the cinnamon. It's an egg envelope to put fillings in.

1. Begin by mixing two eggs (per person) with a splash of milk (one to two tablespoons). Add a little salt and pepper. Stir vigorously with a fork.

2. Add one tablespoon of butter (or cooking oil) to a small frying pan. (Even better is a nonstick pan.) Melt butter over medium heat until bubbly but not burned. Make sure it is spread evenly over the pan.

3. Pour in the egg mixture. As the egg cooks, use a spatula or fork to pull it from the sides to allow the eggs to run underneath. (At the same time you should be shaking the pan. Shaking prevents sticking.)

4. When the omelet has "set," lay the filling on half of it. For filling, save your sweetbreads and capers — grated or crumbled cheddar cheese is child appropriate. (If you want to get *really* fancy, throw in some chopped apple. For other possibilities, see attached map.)

5. Use a spatula to fold the egg over the filling and let the filling melt.

6. Roll the omelet onto a plate—easy to do if you have a slope-sided omelet pan, but an uphill climb if you're cooking in a frying pan.

Dadlike Foodstuffs

Here is a partial list of questionably nutritious but fun-to-make dadlike foods where the kids can pitch in to toss, mix, or stir:

Mixed green salads

Waldorf salad (the one with the apples)

California (onion soup mix) dip

Popcorn

Chex mix

Sloppy Joes

Krispy treats

Chocolate pudding

Caramel apples

Special drinks:

    Fruit juice and seltzer

    Ginger ale and cranberry juice

    Milk shake

    Root beer float

    Limeade

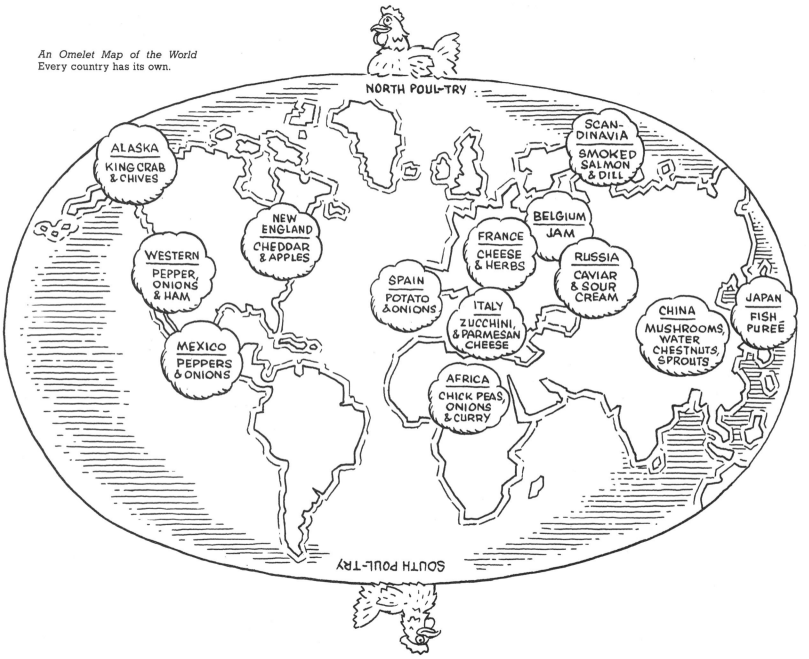

An Omelet Map of the World
Every country has its own.

NORTH POUL-TRY

ALASKA
KING CRAB & CHIVES

SCAN-DINAVIA
SMOKED SALMON & DILL

NEW ENGLAND
CHEDDAR & APPLES

BELGIUM
JAM

FRANCE
CHEESE & HERBS

WESTERN
PEPPER, ONIONS & HAM

RUSSIA
CAVIAR & SOUR CREAM

SPAIN
POTATO & ONIONS

ITALY
ZUCCHINI, & PARMESAN CHEESE

JAPAN
FISH PUREÉ

CHINA
MUSHROOMS, WATER CHESTNUTS, SPROUTS

MEXICO
PEPPERS & ONIONS

AFRICA
CHICK PEAS, ONIONS & CURRY

SOUTH POUL-TRY

How to Fly a Kite

The Kite

My kite goes so
high,
It reaches the sky.

With birdies it
doth play,
Thru the extremely
long day.

Up high it goes
soaring,

It's so very boring.

It dances with the
breeze,

Then crashes in the
trees.

By Helen Joy Green

There never was a page like this in one of your books when you were a child:

The brutal truth is that kite flying is almost always more trouble than it's worth. The secret, therefore, to successful kite flying is to do what you can to shorten the experience.

HOW TO MAKE A KITE

Don't make a kite. It probably wouldn't fly anyway. Buy a kite instead. But don't try to get too fancy.

Diamond-shaped kites are capricious and quirky. Delicate oriental kites love the earth. The kite that is easiest to fly is the delta wing. String on a small spool is hard to hold. Put a stick through it or buy the big spool with handles.

While your child holds the spool, walk about fifty feet downwind with the kite. Ask your child to run away from you. When the string tightens, release the kite. Stop your child from running before he or she disappears and coach him or her to keep the string taut by pulling the slack downward with the nonspool hand.

WIND →

There are two ways to keep a diving kite from getting stuck in a tree: One is to "go with it," that is, move the string in the direction of its plummet and regain control. The other way is to

fly it in a place without trees. The beach is a
place like that. It has, besides, offshore breezes
that can be counted on to blow steadily every
warm summer afternoon.

Other good places are:

How to Make a Paper Airplane

A paper airplane, like a real airplane, can be an instrument of good or evil. It offers the potential for a flight of the imagination or a swift trip to the principal's office.

There are two basic plane plans. The first was the predecessor of the Stealth bomber in design, airworthiness, and speed. It is a delta wing craft requiring five folds.

The second plane is a stubby sort of workhorse design.

- - - - - - - - - - - - FOLD
- - - - - - - - - - - - FOLD
- - - - - - - - - - - - FOLD

A vertical stabilizer may be cut and pushed up, an attractive option that does not discernibly alter performance. Flaps are also an option.

As an instrument of evil, your plane may be flown toward the teacher's desk while her back is turned, or off the balcony at the theater, or some other place where it is likely to cause interruptions and irritation.

As an instrument of good, your plane may be used to deliver smallpox vaccine to the Eskimos, or a love note to Caitlin across the room. (Just be sure to keep it under two hundred words.)

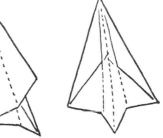

FACES, CAMOUFLAGE, EMBLEMS AND NUMBERS WILL ENHANCE YOUR CRAFT.

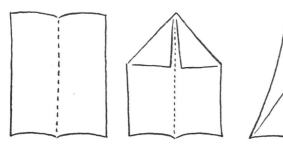

How to Make a Paper Cup, a Cootie Catcher, and a Newspaper Hat

If there is one thing of true worth that is passed on to the next generation, let it be the paper cup. It is ecological. It is magical. Say to a child, "Would you like to drink out of this square of paper?" The astonished, eager child will say, "Yes," and watch with incredulity as you:

FOLD THE SQUARE INTO A TRIANGLE.

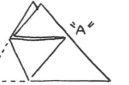

FOLD OVER A CORNER PARALLEL WITH THE BASE, TOUCHING SIDE "A".

DO THE SAME TO THE OTHER SIDE.

TUCK THE FRONT POINT INTO THE LAST CORNER FOLDED OVER.

FOLD THE BACK POINT DOWN.

Sweet Brown LIQUID THAT FOAMS

FILL WITH YOUR CHILDS FAVORITE BEVERAGE.

Note to Dads: Paper cups are used at maker's own risk. Paper used for cup should be unlined and unwritten upon. Otherwise the ink might dissolve into the drink and ruin the whole drinking-from-a-paper-cup experience.

FAIRLY TYPICAL COOTIES

HOW TO MAKE A COOTIE CATCHER

Funnier than lice, less deadly than the deer tick, the cootie has made its home on generations of children. The cootie-infested child is not to be shorn, shampooed, dusted, or dipped. Instead, a cootie catcher must be fashioned to rid the young host of these maliciously grinning vermin.

1. Begin with a square piece of paper. Fold it diagonally.

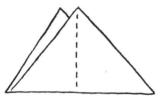

2. Open it and fold it diagonally the other way.

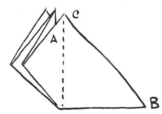

3. Then fold points A and B up to point C.

4. Open it again and re-form it along the folds into a four-pointed star.

5. Put your fingers astride the points so as to control the opening and closing of the two diamonds formed within the star.

6. Draw a cootie in one of the diamonds and close it. Open the other diamond.

You are now ready to inspect for cooties. Holding your catcher poised, advance toward someone's head. Shout "*I see a cootie!*" First make sure to show them the empty diamond, close the catcher on their hair and then pull it away. Open the catcher to reveal the caught cootie. Continue this process until the infestation has been cleared.

HOW TO MAKE A NEWSPAPER HAT

Not only does a newspaper hat offer certain protection from cooties, it also adds a jaunty Gallic air to any child's ensemble. In fact, you will be quite surprised by how many people mistake your child for an eighteenth-century French general.

The ideal newspaper hat is actually made from a standard-size sheet of typing paper because you get a nice tight crease that gives the hat its hold. Unfortunately, if your child's head is any larger than an orange, it is not going to fit.

Choose instead a folded-in-the-middle section from your local newspaper, but no more than six or eight pages or you'll run into that crease problem.

Tabloid-size newspapers can also be used, but avoid headlines like THE AMAZING FROG BABY or I HAD BIGFOOT'S CHILD. The stock market or real estate section will give the hat a businesslike air.

1. With the open side down, fold the upper corners to an imaginary center line and crease like heck.

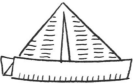

2. Fold up the bottom from both sides.

3. Grip the hat tightly as you pull the sides apart to allow the folds to set.

4. Don't touch anything. Go wash your hands because they are filthy with newsprint.

Now when your child acts like a little dictator, he or she can also look like one.

OPEN UP IN THE NAME OF THE KING!

DO NOT DISTURB

How to Open a Bank Account

Children are built closer to the ground than adults. That makes it easy for them to find a fortune in dropped change and flyaway dollars. Couple this with sales to the Tooth Fairy, lemonade profits, and a hefty allowance and the bottom line is a child with discretionary income. Here lies the opportunity for the father to present the investment options available and their up- and downside risks.

Like many investment counselors, dads may recommend diversification. Therefore it behooves us to know how to open a savings account for our child:

1. You'll need your child's social security number.

2. If you don't have an account at the bank, you'll need to bring a passport, driver's license, or another valid form of ID.

3. You'll also need to bring your child. Some commercial banks require that the child write his or her name on the application.

That's all. If your child is tall enough to reach the teller's desk, he or she can make a deposit, but not a withdrawal. Not until your child turns eighteen. Then he or she can take it all out and invest it in *wanton spending*.

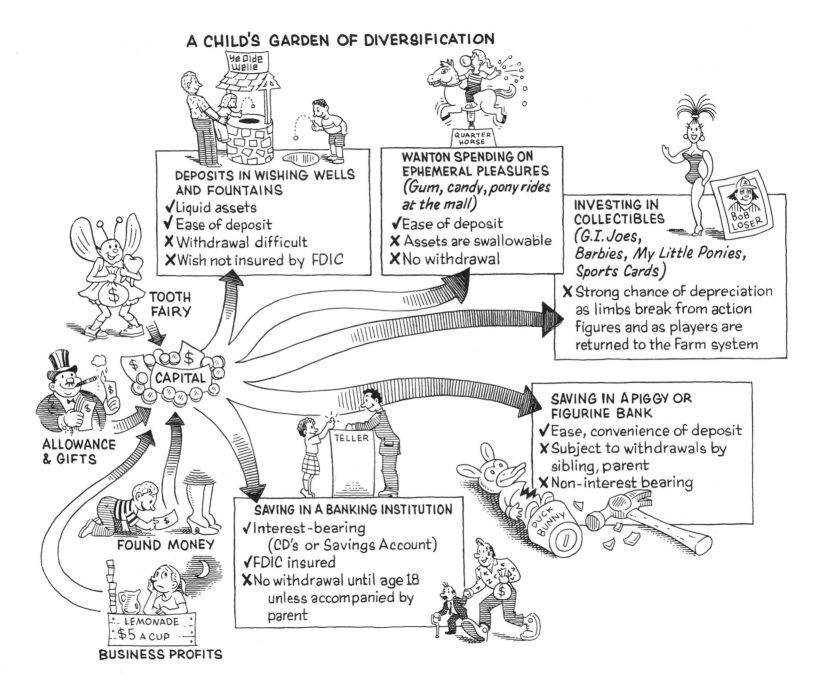

A CHILD'S GARDEN OF DIVERSIFICATION

DEPOSITS IN WISHING WELLS AND FOUNTAINS
- ✓ Liquid assets
- ✓ Ease of deposit
- ✗ Withdrawal difficult
- ✗ Wish not insured by FDIC

WANTON SPENDING ON EPHEMERAL PLEASURES
(Gum, candy, pony rides at the mall)
- ✓ Ease of deposit
- ✗ Assets are swallowable
- ✗ No withdrawal

INVESTING IN COLLECTIBLES
(G.I. Joes, Barbies, My Little Ponies, Sports Cards)
- ✗ Strong chance of depreciation as limbs break from action figures and as players are returned to the Farm system

TOOTH FAIRY

ALLOWANCE & GIFTS

CAPITAL

FOUND MONEY

LEMONADE $5 A CUP

BUSINESS PROFITS

SAVING IN A BANKING INSTITUTION
- ✓ Interest-bearing (CD's or Savings Account)
- ✓ FDIC insured
- ✗ No withdrawal until age 18 unless accompanied by parent

TELLER

SAVING IN A PIGGY OR FIGURINE BANK
- ✓ Ease, convenience of deposit
- ✗ Subject to withdrawals by sibling, parent
- ✗ Non-interest bearing

DUCK BUNNY

How to Stop a Bloody Nose

Serious minded, expensive doctors with second homes tell us that our noses are highly sensitive membranes easily susceptible to outside influence. A drop in humidity, a sudden sneeze, a knuckle sandwich, and just like that, a warm, red dribble begins to course down the valley of the upper lip.

Children are apt to panic at the sight of their own vital fluid spotting their freshly ironed shirt or blouse. Try to calm them by pretending you aren't the least bit panicked yourself or by *diverting their attention.*

The bleeding nose is like a dripping faucet that must be turned off. Tilt the head backward to slow the blood flow and, with thumb and forefinger, pinch the nose just above the nostrils. Hold a tissue below the nostrils until the blood has had a chance to clot—about one or two minutes. The child should remain in the "head-back position," reflecting on all that has come to pass, until the bleeding has completely stopped.

Some sensitive children will pale at the taste of blood and the sight of the caked residue around their nostrils. Wipe their noses, clean and remove all telltale signs of nosebleed before returning them to upright position.

THREE WAYS TO DIVERT ATTENTION

THE "FUNNY" FACE

THE FAKE CRIME

MY SHOES HAVE BEEN STOLEN!

THE FAKE DELIVERY

SOMEONE'S AT THE DOOR!... A PACKAGE?... MARKED "LIVE ANIMALS"?... NO, NOT FOR US... THEY LIVED HERE YEARS AGO... A HORRIBLE THING HAPPENED TO THEM... OKAY, 'BYE!

How to "Father"

Some traditional Norman Rockwellian dadding skills that no longer seem quite right for our time:

How to whittle

How to make a slingshot

How to shoot marbles

How to blow smoke rings

How to build a crystal radio

How to make a magnet/ electric motor

How to make a fire with flint

OTHER CHILDHOOD MEDICAL EMERGENCIES

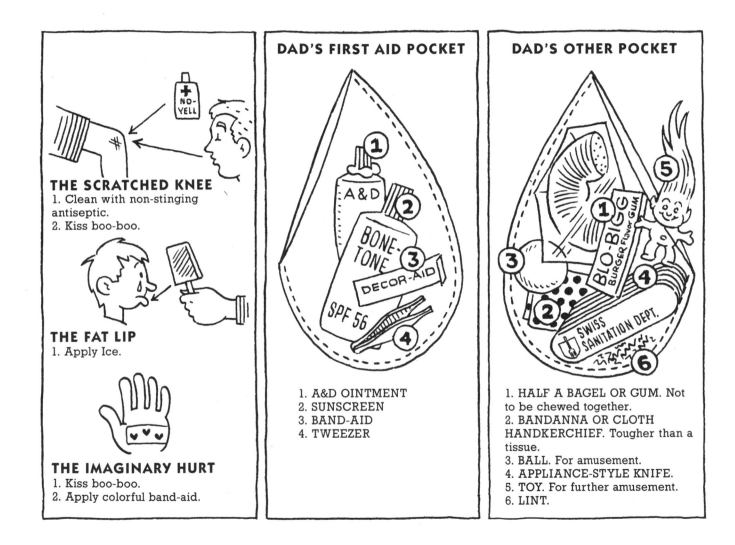

THE SCRATCHED KNEE
1. Clean with non-stinging antiseptic.
2. Kiss boo-boo.

THE FAT LIP
1. Apply Ice.

THE IMAGINARY HURT
1. Kiss boo-boo.
2. Apply colorful band-aid.

DAD'S FIRST AID POCKET

1. A&D OINTMENT
2. SUNSCREEN
3. BAND-AID
4. TWEEZER

DAD'S OTHER POCKET

1. HALF A BAGEL OR GUM. Not to be chewed together.
2. BANDANNA OR CLOTH HANDKERCHIEF. Tougher than a tissue.
3. BALL. For amusement.
4. APPLIANCE-STYLE KNIFE.
5. TOY. For further amusement.
6. LINT.

How to Take a Picture

Look at your family photo album. There is something supernatural going on. Dad is in almost none of the pictures. Actually, that's because Dad is the one taking them.

For better or worse—mostly worse—Dad is usually the family's photographer in residence, and it falls upon him to pass his questionable skills along to his offspring.

In the hopes that your child might become a slightly better photographer than you are, Kodak has provided the following simple tips on how to take better snapshots:

Getting Ready:
—Make sure there's film in the camera.
—Make sure the flash battery is working.
—Make sure you've removed the lens cap.
—Make sure you have enough light.
—Keep your fingers away from the lens.

DAD'S PHOTO ALBUM

IN THE COUNTRY

AT THE BEACH

IN THE PARK

IN THE COUNTRY, AT THE BEACH, IN THE PARK

Taking a Picture:

—Move in close. Better to be too close to your subject than too far away.

—Take pictures of people, but don't shoot groups that are too large.

—Avoid cluttered foregrounds and include only a few things in each picture.

—Don't leave large gaps between subjects.

—Look behind your subject to make sure that the background isn't distracting.

—Capture action. Have people *doing* something.

How to Mow the Lawn, Rake Leaves, and Shovel Snow

Lawn mowing, leaf raking, and snow shoveling have one big thing in common—you see results now! The same cannot be said for most other things done on weekends, except ironing.

Let's consider the full spectrum of human activity from the point of view of the immediate pay-off:

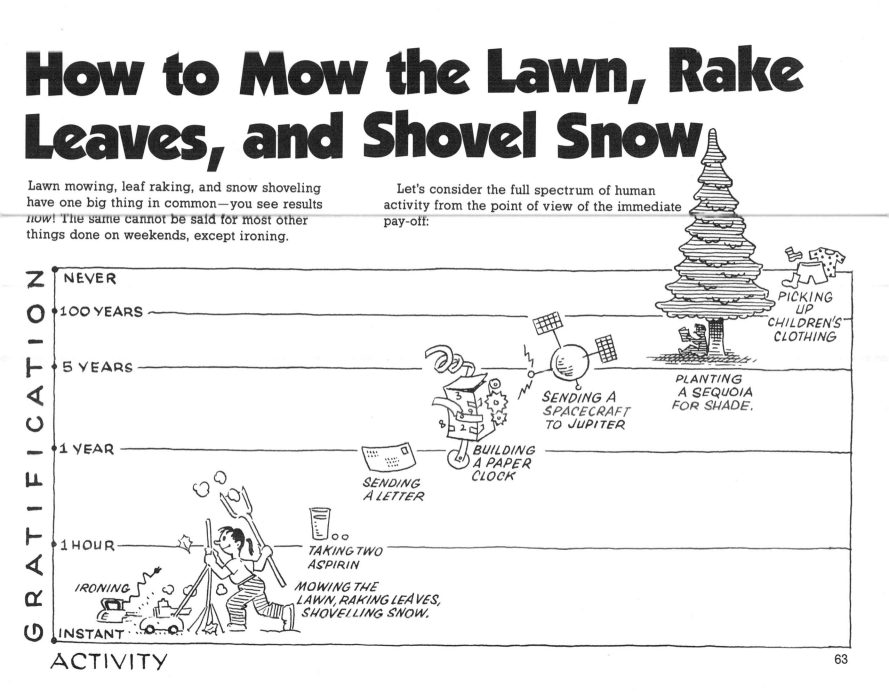

GRATIFICATION

NEVER
100 YEARS
5 YEARS
1 YEAR
1 HOUR
INSTANT

ACTIVITY

PICKING UP CHILDREN'S CLOTHING

PLANTING A SEQUOIA FOR SHADE.

SENDING A SPACECRAFT TO JUPITER

BUILDING A PAPER CLOCK

SENDING A LETTER

TAKING TWO ASPIRIN

IRONING

MOWING THE LAWN, RAKING LEAVES, SHOVELLING SNOW.

63

Lawn mowing, leaf raking, and snow shoveling, the trinity of groundskeeping, are also year-round ways for your child to earn money from you and the neighbors. (Be sure to report this income to the IRS—a prison record will seriously affect your progeny's chances of early admission to the best colleges.)

Lawn mowing, leaf raking, and snow shovelling have three different patters:

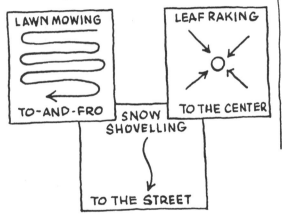

The to-and-fro of mowing should follow overlapping paths to avoid leaving rows of missed grass. Begin at a corner, and if your lawn is a rectangle, travel the long way. This means fewer turns, greater fuel economy and less chance of spinning out. Your child should not operate a mower while medicated or barefoot.

Before your child puts blades to grass, consider the machine. Perhaps you have one or more of these in your fleet:

We would not suggest giving your child the keys to the Grass Avenger unless he/she has successfully completed a driver's ed course. Use of a sit-on mower by an 8-year-old can lead to reckless endangerment and premature harvesting of gardens, shrubs, and small trees.

A hand mower works well for small estates, but since children tire and cry easily, roll out the power mower.

Areas under trees and around shrubs and flamingos are best left to father.

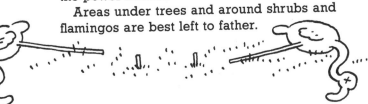

HUP 2, 3, 4!
I LEFT MY WIFE
IN NEW ORLEANS
WITH 48 KIDS
AND A CAN
OF BEANS.
HUP, HUP...

LEAF RAKING

Leaf raking has a byproduct as well, a pile of leaves that crunches like a bowl of cornflakes. It is part of every father's genetic baggage to know how to fall face down into this pile. And it is part of every child's genetic baggage to fall on top of him.

Leaf raking is done toward a series of centers on the lawn. In each center is a bag. The leaves are stuffed into the bag and the child is placed on top. Ask the child to march. This compacting action actually reduces leaf occupancy space by one-third!

If you take your leaf bags to a landfill, empty them and re-use the bags. Thank you for reducing environmental impact.

SNOW SHOVELLING

The snow shoveller also has a formidable arsenal to choose from: snow blowers, snow throwers, snow plows, and snow shovels. The shovel is the simplest to operate, yet you've surely heard of thousands maimed and immobilized because they've shovelled with their backs.

THE TAI-CHI OF SNOW SHOVELLING

Instead of his/her back, the shoveller should use the earth. By planting one leg rearwards and pushing backwards against the ground as you move forward with the shovel, the resistance "travels up" through the shovel and down through the leg "into" the earth. You've got the whole globe behind you.

A TRIANGLE IS MORE STRUCTURAL ...THAN A SHLUMP.

WHICH WAY TO GO

If shovelling is begun at the street end of a walk it will trap the occupants of the house inside until a thaw. So the rule is: ALWAYS SHOVEL TOWARD THE STREET.

The snow should be thrown on the lawn, not into the street where it would lie as a trap for a car leaving the garage.

Finally, it is an immutable law of the universe than when every last driveway on the block has been shovelled out, a plow shall appear and bury them all.

How to Build a Campfire

No man will ever look smaller in his child's burning eyes than when, in the middle of the darkening wildwood, he builds a choking column of smoke instead of a fire. In vain he will try to convince his child that marshmallows, like turkey breasts, ham, and salmon, taste better when smoked.

If only he had memorized this homespun little poem by Ernest Thompson Seton, America's first Chief Scout:

1. Find a curl of birchwood as dry as it can be,
2. Then some twigs of softwood, dead, but on the tree,
3. Last of all some pine knots to make the kittle foam,
4. An' thar's a fire to make ye think yer sittin' right at home.

Let's analyze this bit of verse: Line 1 is the tinder. Line 2 is the kindling. Line 3 is the fuel. Line 4 is to make it rhyme.

These are the ingredients of a successful fire. The match lights the tinder, the tinder lights the kindling, the kindling lights the fuel, the fuel burns the marshmallow.

MATCH	→ TINDER	→ KINDLING	→ FUEL	→ MARSHMALLOW
	DEAD BIRCHBARK, DEAD GRAPEVINES, DRY WEEDTOPS	SMALL STICKS FOUND ON DEAD TREES OR THE GROUND	DEAD BRANCHES BUFFALO CHIPS	

A fire is built. These are the building materials. Now let's look at the architecture.

THE LEAN-TO

Find a fire stick (a green stick), and push it into the ground pointing into the wind. Put some tinder under it. Then lean some kindling against the fire stick. Over the kindling lay fuel. Light the tinder at the open end.

A variation on this uses two rocks to support the fire stick.

REMEMBER, FOLKS, A FIRE BUILT ON ROCK OR GRAVEL IS THE SAFEST OF ALL. IF YOU CAN'T DO THAT, BE SURE TO CLEAR ALL FLAMMABLE MATERIAL WITHIN A TEN-FOOT CIRCLE OF YOUR FIRE. DROWN YOUR FIRE WHEN YOU'RE DONE. TURN OVER ALL STICKS AND LOGS AND DRENCH THEM ON BOTH SIDES. FINALLY, BURY THE ASHES. *REMEMBER, ONLY <u>YOU</u> CAN PREVENT FATHER FIRES!*

How to Row a Boat

IT'S LIKE DOING THE BREAST STROKE WITHOUT LOOKING WHERE YOU'RE GOING.

TITANIC BOAT RENTAL

JUMP TIMMY!

Sometimes you believed your father was the strongest, smartest man in the world. And one of those times was probably when he rowed you across a lake. Your belief was confirmed when he let you take an oar. The boat slowed and moved into a hopeless little circle.

WHAT HE KNEW THAT YOU DIDN'T

Rowing is like swimming the breaststroke. Oars equal arms. Boat equals body. Arms reach forward out of the water and go into the water and push the water behind. The body goes forward.

Hold the oars by the narrow ends and bend forward, extending your arms as though you were bowing to your children. Keep the wide ends (the "hands") in the air. Then let them slice, never splash, into the water. Now begin to sit up and pull the narrow ends toward you, angling the "hands" to maximize their push of the water away from you.

Stop before your fists crush your muscular, hairy chest. Now push down to lift the "hands" from the water, and in an easy, continuous motion, bend forward, and bow once more to your children.

WHAT YOUR CHILD CAN SEE THAT YOU CAN'T

One of the drawbacks to rowing a boat is that you are sitting with your back to the direction in which you are moving.

Therefore, if your children are screaming hysterically, consider the following possibilities:

SOMETHING'S IN THE WAY.

YOU'RE THERE ALREADY.

THEY'RE JUST PLAIN NERVOUS.

You must glance over your shoulder occasionally to assess your course. Once you've established your objective, line one of your children's heads up with a fixed object on the distant shore. Keep the two together and you'll remain on course.

NAVIGATIONAL METHOD

THE SECRET OF TURNING

When your child takes the oars, he or she will usually let one fall into the water. Notice what happens as the left oar floats downstream and your child continues to row with the right: The boat turns to the right. Just the opposite happens if your child loses the right oar. Learn about turning from this experience.

WHAT THE ROMAN EMPIRE KNEW THAT YOU DIDN'T

Take a tip from slave ship movies—grease your body and stand in the back of the boat. Clap two blocks of wood together or strike a large gong with a hammer. It helps your child develop a good rowing rhythm and presents an impressive sight to those on the shore.

Note to Dads: Don't try to adopt a salty air when teaching your child to row. Avoid tattooing anchors on your chest. Avoid calling your child "matey" or "bilge puppy." Avoid the wearing of anchovies. Children are quick to spot a phony.

How to Carve Soap

If Michelangelo had had bath-size bars of Ivory soap available to him, he certainly would have preferred them to blocks of Carrara marble. Let's look at the evidence:

SOAP VS. MARBLE AS A SCULPTURAL MEDIUM

	SOAP	MARBLE
Can be carved with a penknife	✓	
Can use chips in driveway or patio		✓
Can use chips to wash clothes	✓	
Sculpture floats in your bathtub	✓	
Requires no expensive chisels or hammers	✓	
You don't have to go to Carrara	✓	
Total	**5**	**1**

GETTING STARTED

Select a well-sharpened penknife (although with Ivory soap even a blunt butter knife will do) and then review the *Cardinal Rule of Soap Carving:*

Never carve toward yourself. To reinforce the message, show your child this cautionary picture of a youth who did not obey the *Cardinal Rule of Soap Carving.*

Next, using a stylus or toothpick, make a sketch of your subject on the bar of soap.

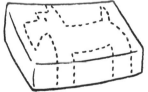

Choose from animal, vegetable, or people themes. Simple, stocky subjects work best. A Scottie dog, a squatty duck, or an Eastern European would be a good choice. A flock of hummingbirds, a DNA molecule, or the Battle of Gettysburg would be poor choices for a beginner.

Now start hacking away.

REFINEMENTS

After the initial hacking-away phase, refine the sculpture by shaving it with your knife.

Further refining can be accomplished by rubbing with a damp piece of cheesecloth. Remember to save the chips for your laundry.

When the sculpture looks complete, you are ready for the unveiling. Place it on display or in the bathtub. Add some rope for the shower.

A FINAL NOTE OF CAUTION: Michelangelo could exhibit his work outdoors; you can't.

MAN WITH A HOE

How to Build a Sand Castle

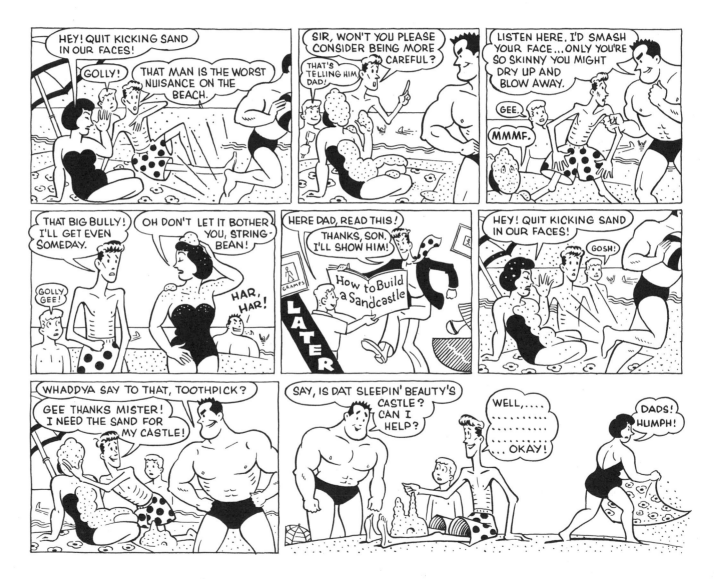

Waterfront property has its risks. As coastal erosion moves our shorelines relentlessly inland, tune up now for that sense of loss by building a sand castle.

Build your dream castle between the high-water mark and the surf. If the tide is going out, the castle will be reduced to a vacant lot in a matter of hours. An incoming tide will take even less time. A volleyball game, exercising the right of eminent domain, will level it even faster.

SITE SELECTION

Choose a location near the high-tide mark. You can locate the high-tide mark by looking for a line of stranded mermaids, medical waste, and the two sams: flot and jet.

PLANNING

Choose from one of the two basic plans:

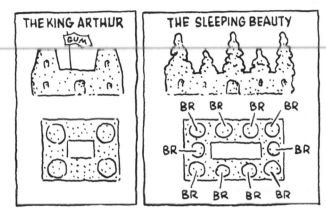

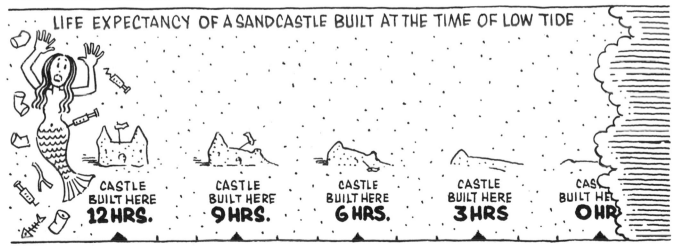

LIFE EXPECTANCY OF A SANDCASTLE BUILT AT THE TIME OF LOW TIDE

CASTLE BUILT HERE **12 HRS.**

CASTLE BUILT HERE **9 HRS.**

CASTLE BUILT HERE **6 HRS.**

CASTLE BUILT HERE **3 HRS**

CAS BUILT HE **O HR**

CONSTRUCTION

Draw the outline of the foundation in the sand. Scoop out a ditch in the shape of the outline, placing the sand in a pile in the center. The ditch is the moat. Shape the pile into a square doughnut. The hole is the central courtyard where the peasantry can seek refuge when Vikings pillage the beach.

Build up the walls and level the tops. For the King Arthur model, pack moist sand into a pail of appropriate size or half a milk carton. Turn it over on one of the four corners. Tap the bottom and remove it. Do the same on the other three corners. Call these lumps "towers."

The construction technique employed for Sleeping Beauty's tower dazzles beachgoers: it is the Dribble Method.

Fill your hand with wet, runny sand. Make a fist and turn your hand so your thumb is up, pinky down. Let the sand dribble through the hole between pinky and palm. (Paper cups filled with runny sand can also be used.)

With a little practice and by applying successive layers of dribble, you will be able to create fantastic towers in the tradition of Mad King Ludwig of Bavaria. The Dribble Method can also be used to make fir trees with which to dot the castle's broad lawns.

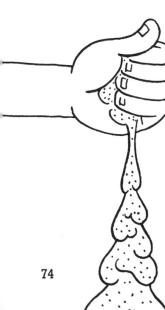

FINISHING

Castle contractors should consult this checklist:

DON'T FORGET
- ☐ DRAWBRIDGE
- ☐ PARAPETS
- ☐ SLIT WINDOWS
- ☐ BANNER

When your sand castle is completed, you may wish to consider some additions:

A TWO-CLAM GARAGE

FINISH THE ATTIC FOR THE KIDS

A DUNGEON (NOTE MUSSEL TORTURING A PERIWINKLE)

TOLL PLAZA, SHOWING DEAD CRABS AND
CLAMSHELLS APPROACHING BEVERAGE CAN
TOLL BOOTHS. NOTE CRAB WITH EXACT CHANGE.

HOW TO DIG A TUNNEL

As with castle construction, site selection is
important here. A tunnel dug near the surf will
flood and collapse. Begin by choosing where the
ends of the tunnel are to be and dig in. Dig
deep to minimize the chances of a cave-in. Use
your hands. If your fingertips turn raw, use a
clamshell or a plastic shovel or even a pail.

If you dig with a partner from opposite ends,
you will be able to experience the great
transcendent moment in sandhoggery. It occurs
when the last bit of wall between digging
partners is broken through and they touch new
fingertips.

You may wish to add a toll plaza at one end of
the tunnel. You can also decorate the facade of
the tunnel (the place where the trailer truck
gets wedged) in an artful way with pieces of
shell and other seaborne debris.

CAUTION: Remember the film *Corfam the Jungle Boy*?
How the hunter in search of the Graveyard
of the Elephants was swallowed up by
quicksand? Well, if you stand above the
route of the tunnel, that will happen to you.
Be sure to scream as you are sucked
under.

How to Make a Snowman

The snowman was synonymous with winters before the greenhouse effect eliminated most snow south of the Arctic Circle. If you are blessed with a snowfall, however, it will most likely be wet and sticky, rather than dry and powdery. While wet snow makes all other aspects of life miserable, it is the preferred medium for snowmen.

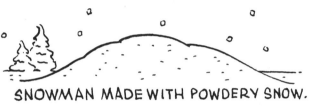

SNOWMAN MADE WITH POWDERY SNOW.

THE BASIC THREE-BALL MAN
Begin by making a softball-size, firmly packed snowball. Then roll it in the snow, changing the axis of the ball as you go so you do not roll a snow log. Make three balls, small, medium, and

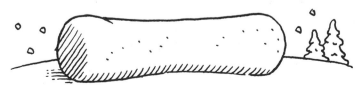

IMPROPER ROLLING OF BALL

IMPROPER STACKING OF ELEMENTS

large. Stack them properly. Flatten them where they touch, adding snow "mortar" to enhance their bonding.

Now it's time for your snowman to go to makeup and wardrobe.

CUSTOMIZING
Find small, dark objects to use for the eyes and mouth. A carrot is the traditional nose, but any root crop will do. Green, leafy vegetables, such as lettuce, although excellent nutritionally, make a poor nose. Add sticks for arms.

WRONG: LETTUCE NOSE

You would be wise to forget about putting your snowman in pants. Jackets will fit poorly, draping excessively on his rounded shoulders and thin arms. A bespoke jacket would be best, perhaps in a hearty twenty-four-ounce Donegal tweed. Hats, scarves, and gloves add a jaunty note. As do shoes.

How to Carve a Pumpkin

Because Halloween only comes once a year, carving a pumpkin is one of those dad-intensive labors that always seems less laborious than it actually is.

CHOOSING A PUMPKIN

So don't be a hero. Leave those giant hormone-injected pumpkins to the pumpkin-carving professionals. Choose instead a basketball-size pumpkin in one of two basic shapes—either oblong for that Edvard Munch look, or the classic squatty jack-o'-lantern shape. (A pumpkin doesn't have to be perfect all around, but choose one with enough smooth surface for the face.)

HAPPY
HALLOWEEN
by
Edvard
Munch

COURTESY METROPOLITAN MUSEUM OF PIE FILLINGS

HOLLOWING IT OUT

To carve a pumpkin, use a sharp serrated knife (a steak knife will do). Begin by removing the top of the pumpkin's head. Cut out a circle around the stem about eight inches in diameter. Before removing the top make a mark across the cut that can be matched up (so that it won't take you five minutes every time to find the proper fit) when you replace it. A second smaller concentric circle should be cut around the stem or "hat" so that it can be removed when the candle is lit.

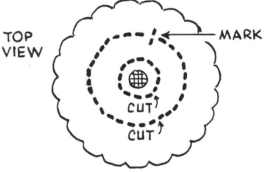

TOP VIEW

MARK

CUT

CUT

Remove the seeds and the pulp with the biggest spoon you have (here's where the kids can help). Both the pulp (in pies) and the seeds (salted and toasted) are technically edible, but as a culinary experience, neither is worth the effort. Scrape away part of the inner side of the shell where you plan to put the face to abet cutting.

78

MAKING A FACE

Again, keep it simple—either the Edvard Munch look or the classic, as illustrated.

Make a dotted line with a felt-tip pen to approximate the face you want to carve. Start by making a dot just above what you envision to be the top of the nose. This is the midpoint of the face, which will help you give the face a balanced perspective.

To give your pumpkin a more menacing look, draw geometric eyebrows, slant the eye triangles inward, and give the mouth a more carved look.

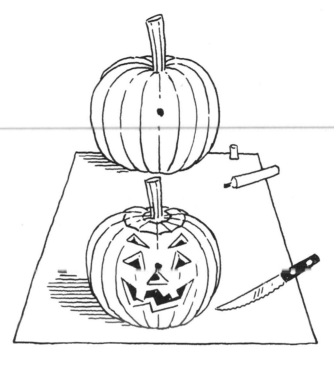

LIGHTING THE CANDLE

Push down a candle to mush out a little hole in the pulp at the bottom of the pumpkin. Light the candle, and tilt it so that the little hole is filled with melted wax. Stick the candle in the melted wax and allow it to set.

DON'T BE A HERO.

U-PICK 'EM

How to Change a Diaper

This final chapter is the only activity in the book where the participating child is supposed to remain utterly passive (even if he or she almost never does). However, no book of modern dad skills would be complete without instructions for changing a baby's diaper.

Fortunately, the near-total extinction of cloth diapers has made the whole process pretty much a no-brainer anyway. But even with paper diapers there are still three things you need to remember:

1. Diapers come in three sizes—small, medium, and large (the boxes are color-coded). Make sure your baby falls within the approximate weight range stated on the box. If you don't know your baby's weight, follow this chart.

Newborn: Small
Smallish baby: Medium
Biggish baby: Large

2. If the baby has ... you know, don't forget the wipes.

3. Put the side with the sticky tape *under* the baby. There is one final important technique you should be aware of when the baby has made a ... you know. While holding the baby up by its legs and after wiping the bottom clean, place the dirty wipes inside the dirty diaper, *then fold the diaper over* before reaching for a clean one. That way, if the baby starts to squirm, you won't have a real mess on your hands or on the changing table.

THIS GUY'S GONNA TEACH ME HOW TO RIDE A BIKE?